FIESTA!

CHINA

GROLIER
EDUCATIONAL

Published for Grolier Educational
Sherman Turnpike, Danbury, Connecticut
by Marshall Cavendish Books
an imprint of Times Media Pte Ltd
Times Centre, 1 New Industrial Road, Singapore 536196
Tel: (65) 2848844 Fax: (65) 2854871
Email: te@corp.tpl.com.sg
World Wide Web:
http://www.timesone.com.sg/te

Set ISBN: 0-7172-9099-9
Volume ISBN: 0-7172-9112-X

Library of Congress Cataloging-in-Publication Data
China.
p.cm. -- (Fiesta!)
Summary: Discusses the festivals of China and how their songs, recipes, and traditions
reflect the culture of the people.
ISBN 0-7172-9112-X (hardbound)
1. Festivals -- China -- Juvenile literature. 2. China -- Social life and customs -- Juvenile literature.
[1. Festivals -- China. 2. China -- Social life and customs.]
I. Series: Fiesta! (Danbury, Conn.)
GT4883.A2C4912 1997
394.26951--dc21
97-5261
CIP
AC

Marshall Cavendish Books Editorial Staff
Editorial Director: Ellen Dupont
Series Designer: Joyce Mason
Crafts devised and created by Susan Moxley
Music arrangements by Harry Boteler
Photographs by Bruce Mackie
Subeditors: Susan Janes, Judy Fovargue
Production: Craig Chubb

For this volume
Editor: Susie Dawson
Designer: Trevor Vertigan
Consultant: Xiaoyun Yao
Editorial Assistant: Bindu Mathur

Printed in Italy

Adult supervision advised for all crafts and recipes
particularly those involving sharp instruments and heat.

CONTENTS

CHINA:

China has more people than any other country. It is the third largest country after the Russian Federation and Canada.

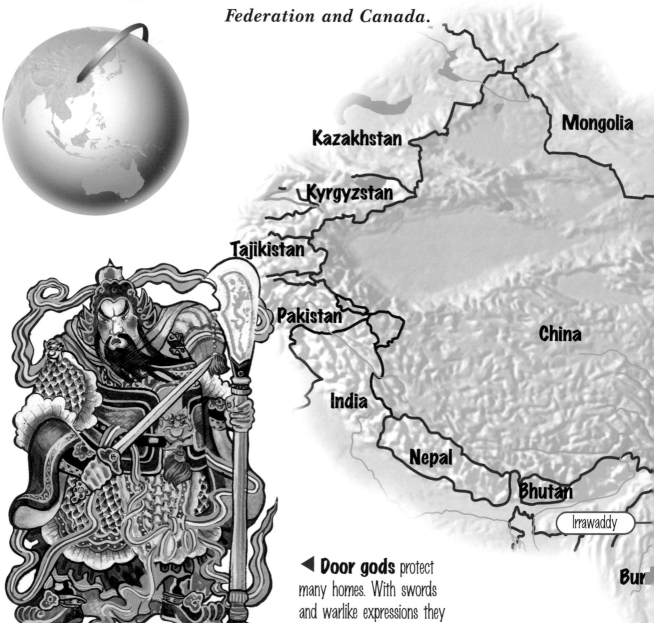

Kazakhstan

Mongolia

Kyrgyzstan

Tajikistan

Pakistan

China

India

Nepal

Bhutan

Irrawaddy

Bur

◀ **Door gods** protect many homes. With swords and warlike expressions they keep away evil spirits.

4

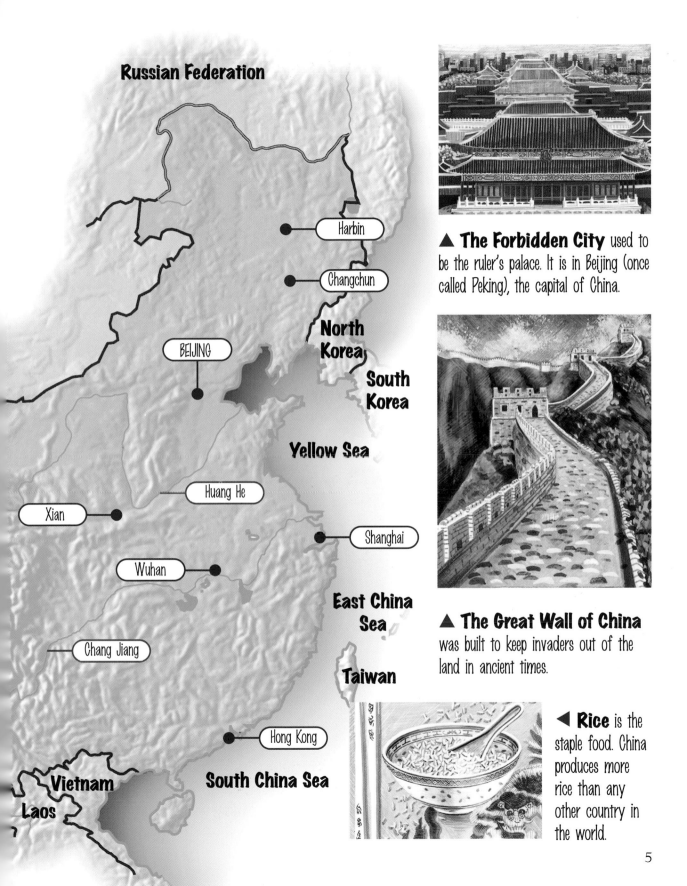

Russian Federation

Harbin

Changchun

North Korea

South Korea

BEIJING

Yellow Sea

Huang He

Xian

Shanghai

Wuhan

East China Sea

Chang Jiang

Taiwan

Hong Kong

Vietnam

Laos

South China Sea

▲ **The Forbidden City** used to be the ruler's palace. It is in Beijing (once called Peking), the capital of China.

▲ **The Great Wall of China** was built to keep invaders out of the land in ancient times.

◀ **Rice** is the staple food. China produces more rice than any other country in the world.

5

RELIGIONS

Most people in China believe in a mixture of three different religions – Confucianism, Taoism, and Buddhism. Each can be practiced alongside the others.

Chinese people use traditions from many different religions and folk beliefs in their religious ceremonies. Buddhism, Taoism, and Confucianism are all included. None of these religions claims to be the one and only truth, so each of them can be practiced together

In Chinese legend the lion is a symbol of bravery. It is the protector of sacred buildings, and its statue often stands outside them.

This jade statue is of a female god. Jade is treasured for bringing health, good luck, and long life.

with the others. Chinese people do not attend regular weekly religious services.

There are minorities in northwest China that practice Islam, while small groups of Christians exist, mainly in the larger cities.

CONFUCIANISM takes its name from the Chinese philosopher Confucius, who lived in the 6th century B.C. His writings advise people how to behave: Everyone should be considerate of others, should respect their ancestors, and should avoid extreme behavior. He claimed that if people did as he said, everyone would be able to live in peace.

BUDDHISM was started in India about 2,500 years ago by a man who became known as the Buddha. "Buddha" means "the enlightened one," and he was called this because he was very wise. The teachings of Buddha reached China about 500 years later. Buddhists in China are called Mahayana Buddhists. They believe that Buddha can answer requests from people today. They also see him as one of many Buddhas of the past, present, and future.

TAOISM was founded about the same time as Buddhism by a Chinese man called Lao-tzu. Taoists believe there are two opposite forces in all things in the world. They call these forces yin and yang. Yin stands for female, passive, and dark. Yang stands for male, active, and light. It is only when these forces are in balance that harmony can be achieved.

GREETINGS FROM **CHINA!**

China has more people than any other country in the world. The majority of the people speak Mandarin Chinese, which is the national language. There are also more than 50 different ethnic groups, many of which have their own customs and some of them their own language. Since the rise to power of the Communist Party in 1949, many of China's old customs and traditions have been swept aside. In the countryside, however, many have survived. Chinese communities in other parts of the world also continue to keep alive the old ways.

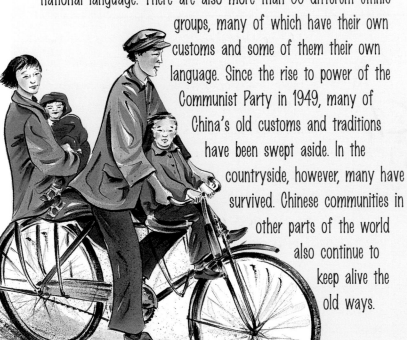

How do you say...

Hello
Ni Hao

Goodbye
Zai jian

Thank you
Xie xie

Peace
He ping

CHINESE NEW YEAR

The New Year according to the Chinese lunar calendar is the most widely celebrated festival in China. It is now called the Spring Festival.

At the time of Chinese New Year poems are written on long strips of red paper and hung outside doorways to ensure good luck for the coming year.

The Chinese New Year takes place between January 21 and February 20. The exact date changes from year to year. Like most other traditional Chinese festivals its date depends on the Chinese lunar calendar. In this calendar each month begins with the new moon.

Preparations go on for several days before the festival starts. The New Year is very much seen as a time of new beginnings. For this reason everyone cleans the house and buys new clothes. All debts should be paid and arguments resolved. People make sure that their kitchen is extra clean. The Chinese believe that before New Year the kitchen god reports back to the higher gods on the family's behavior during the year. His lips are rubbed with honey to make sure he says sweet things.

Large pictures of fierce gods are pasted onto doors or gates to

Paper cutouts in red paper are hung in windows as part of New Year decorations.

8

MAKE A DRAGON

Dragon dances are held at the time of Chinese New Year. The dragon is a symbol of good fortune, so a visit from the dragon will bring good luck.

Both dragon and lion dances are performed at any festive occasion in China. For the lion dance only two people are needed, but for the dragon there can be a whole long line under the material. Sometimes the dragon just dances around trying to catch a pearl that is held up in front of it. Sometimes a game is played in which the head tries to catch the tail.

Whatever the occasion a visit from the dragon or the lion always brings good luck.

MAKING THE PEARL

To make the pearl, blow up a small balloon. Using wallpaper paste, stick several layers of newspaper over it and leave it to dry. Paint the pearl and leave it to dry. Attach the pearl to the top of a small pole. Decorate the pole with material or colored tissue paper.

YOU WILL NEED

Small cardboard boxes
Empty toilet paper tubes
Newspaper • Wallpaper paste
Poster paints
Long, thin, flexible branches
Length of material • Tissue paper

1 Construct the dragon's head using an assortment of cardboard boxes. The nostrils and eyes can be made with empty toilet paper tubes. Tape everything securely in place. Paste strips of newspaper over the surface.

2 Shape the horns from twisted rolls of newspaper and stick them on the back of the dragon's head. Cut a tongue out of cardboard and cover that with strips of newspaper too. Paint over the newspaper with white paint. When the paint is dry, draw your design for the final paintwork in pencil over the top of the white paint. Using whatever colors you choose, paint the final design on the dragon's head.

3 To prepare the body, cut a piece of material. The length of it depends on how many people are going to be inside. Each person needs a thin, flexible branch to hold. Sew the material to the branches. Cut tassels of colored tissue paper and sew them to both material and branches.

ZODIAC ANIMALS

The Chinese zodiac follows a 12-year cycle. Each year is named after an animal.

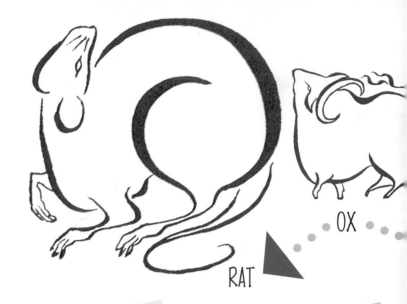

OX

RAT

Along, long time ago, the emperor of the heavens held a race to decide how the years should be named. All the animals took part in a competition to see what names the years should have and in which order they should come.

The race was held across a river. In the end it was the rat who won by tricking the ox into giving him a ride on his back. The other animals arrived in the order shown here. The cat came in thirteenth place, which is why it has never been honored by having a year named after it.

RAT
February 15, 1972 - February 2, 1973
February 2, 1984 - February 19, 1985
February 19, 1996 - February 6, 1997

Charming and quick-witted, Rats love conversation and are good at solving problems.

OX
February 3, 1973 - January 22, 1974
February 20, 1985 - February 8, 1986
February 7, 1997 - January 27, 1998

Stubborn and reliable, Ox types will work at something until it is completely finished.

DRAGON
January 31, 1976 - February 17, 1977
February 17, 1988 - February 5, 1989
February 5, 2000 - January 23, 2001

Brilliant and imaginative, Dragons are usually one step ahead of everyone else.

SNAKE
February 18, 1977 - February 6, 1978
February 6, 1989 - January 26, 1990
January 24, 2001 - February 11, 2002

Quiet, elegant, and clever, Snakes have a reputation for wisdom and good sense.

MONKEY
February 16, 1980 - February 4, 1981
February 4, 1992 - January 22, 1993
January 22, 2004 - February 8, 2005

Lively and unpredictable, the mischievous Monkey is always causing trouble.

ROOSTER
February 5, 1981 - January 24, 1982
January 23, 1993 - February 9, 1994
February 9, 2005 - January 28, 2006

Stylish and flamboyant, Roosters are perfectionists who live life to the full.

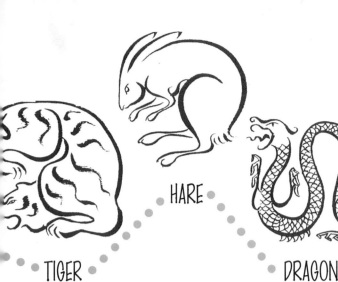

HARE

SNAKE

DRAGON

TIGER

HORSE

RAM

MONKEY

ROOSTER

DOG

PIG

TIGER
January 23, 1974 - February 10, 1975
February 9, 1986 - January 28, 1987
January 28, 1998 - February 15, 1999

Brave, self-confident, and forceful, Tigers have excellent leadership qualities.

HARE
February 11, 1975 - January 30, 1976
January 29, 1987 - February 16, 1988
February 16, 1999 - February 4, 2000

Kind and considerate, Hares love to help people and have a natural gift for healing.

HORSE
February 7, 1978 - January 27, 1979
January 27, 1990 - February 14, 1991
February 12, 2002 - January 31, 2003

Helpful and trustworthy, Horses love people and have boundless amounts of energy.

RAM
January 28, 1979 - February 15, 1980
February 15, 1991 - February 3, 1992
February 1, 2003 - January 21, 2004

Thoughtful and artistic, Rams will do well at anything that requires a lot of patience.

DOG
January 25, 1982 - February 12, 1983
February 10, 1994 - January 30, 1995
January 29, 2006 - February 17, 2007

Friendly, funny, and loyal, people born in the year of the Dog make perfect friends.

PIG
February 13, 1983 - February 1, 1984
January 31, 1995 - February 18, 1996
February 18, 2007 - February 6, 2008

Easy-going, happy, and warm-hearted, Pigs love a quiet, comfortable life.

QING MING

This festival was originally a celebration of the return of spring and the end of winter.

The start of spring is signaled by the festival of Qing Ming, which falls on April 4 or 5. Many Chinese go on picnics and on trips to the countryside. They fly kites and admire the beauty of nature. Qing Ming literally means "pure brightness."

On this day people also go to graves and pay their respects to their ancestors. They clean the area around the graves, light candles,

hao yi duo me-i-li de mo-li- hua

fen - fang mei - li —— man zhi ya

you bai —— you xiang —— ren - ren —— kua

rang —— wo —— lai jiang ni zhai —— xia

song ge-i bie —— ren —— jia mo- li

1. 2.

hua ya mo- li - hua hua

JASMINE FLOWER

What a beautiful jasmine flower,
What a beautiful jasmine flower,
Fragrant, pretty, on the branch,
White and fragrant, praised by all,
Let me pick a jasmine flower
To give to someone,
Jasmine flower, jasmine flower!

and burn incense. They may offer food as well. Often paper money and paper imitations of a variety of goods are burned. It is believed that by burn-ing all t h e s e things, the living can make sure that the dead have everything they need in the next world.

The practice of visiting graves on this day had become less common in the last half of the 20th century. Now it is getting more popular again.

The objects shown here are paper imitations of the real things. It is thought that burning imitation money, clothes, and goods at the graveside will make sure that dead relatives have everything they need in the afterlife.

17

YIDAHAN DEFEATS THE DEMON

The Dai people live in the southwest of China. In April every year they hold a festival in which water is splashed over everyone. It is their way of honoring the courage of a young girl named Yidahan and of keeping bad spirits away for the coming year.

LONG, LONG AGO there lived a fierce and evil demon who caused the local Dai people great suffering. He was a huge giant who breathed wind and fire from his mouth.

He captured seven beautiful maidens from the village. They all hated him and spent their time thinking up ways of killing him. One of them, whose name was Yidahan, thought up a plan to do away with the demon for ever. She entertained the demon with a lavish feast and made sure he drank a lot of wine. In his merry state he talked and talked. He told the girl his great secret.

"I have one weak point that no one knows about. If someone pulls a hair off my head and tightens it around my neck, my neck will be cut through and I will drop down dead. But please don't tell anyone."

While the demon slept, Yidahan carefully pulled out one of his hairs and wound it around his neck. Instantly the devil's head was rolling around on the ground. But wherever it rolled, it set things on fire. Houses, crops, and even people went up in flames. Yidahan grabbed the demon's head and held it still. The other six girls rushed to the river and brought water to put out the fire. They sprinkled it over Yidahan. The fires gradually went out. The demon had been killed and Yidahan had saved the people from their terror.

DRAGON BOAT FESTIVAL

This festival is held in the middle of summer.
It began as a way of trying to please the
dragon who lived in the river.

People often get sick at the hottest time of the year, because germs breed faster in the heat. The festival began as a way to keep people safe from disease and make sure the dragon who lived in the river remained friendly. His goodwill was important since it was he who controlled the rain.

In more recent times the festival came to be a commemoration of the death of the poet Qu Yuan, who lived over 2,000 years ago. He threw himself into the river because he thought

FRUIT SALAD

SERVES 4
2 or 3 pieces preserved ginger
in syrup
8 ounces litchis
1 piece watermelon

1 Reserve 4 tbsp ginger syrup. Cut ginger into long, thin strips; set aside.
2 Use your fingers to peel off the litchis' red shells. Cut litchis in half and remove seeds. Remove watermelon seeds.

3 Use a teaspoon to scoop into balls. Put into a bowl. Stir in litchis, ginger, and syrup. Chill until ready to serve.

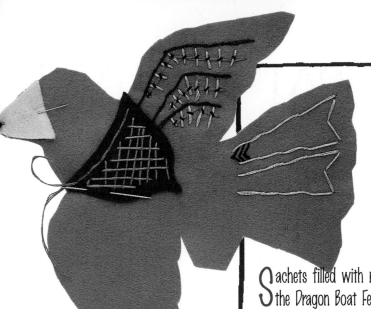

HERBAL SACHETS

YOU WILL NEED

Colored felt
Embroidery thread
Embroidery needles
Pipe cleaners
Absorbent cotton or scented herbs

Sachets filled with medicinal herbs are given to people at the time of the Dragon Boat Festival. The herbs are intended to ward off disease, and the sachets are hung up at home or pinned to clothes.

1 Draw your design for the outline onto some paper. Cut it out, then pin it on two layers of felt, and cut around the paper pattern.

2 In contrasting colors cut out shapes to be sewn as decoration on top of the original ones (for example, the bird's beak).

3 Lightly draw your embroidery design in pen on the felt. Then embroider over the top. Sew the extra bits of felt in place.

4 Sew the sides together. Leave a small gap at the end. Loosely fill the sachet with absorbent cotton or a scented herb.

the rulers were cruel and unfair. People tried to save him but were too late. They then threw rice cakes into the water to stop the river dragon from eating his body.

Ever since then rice cakes, called *zong zi*, wrapped in bamboo leaves tied up with colored thread, have been eaten at the festival.

People also race long, narrow rowing boats in memory of the effort to save him. The boats have carved dragon heads on the prow and are rowed by dozens of people.

MOON FESTIVAL

This festival is held on the day of the full moon in midautumn. On this day the moon is farthest from the earth and at its brightest.

In the mythology of China the moon has always been linked with yin, which represents feminine nature, while the sun is seen as yang, or masculine. It is for this reason that the Moon Festival is most often celebrated by women.

Many years ago offerings were made to the moon on this day. Altars were set up with a statue of the rabbit that the Chinese see in the moon or a picture of the moon palace. Fruit was put on plates. Round fruit such as peaches, grapes, and melons were selected to represent the shape of the moon. There were also 13 mooncakes, one for each month of the

Children carry multicolored lanterns through the streets in the evening. The lanterns shown here are in the shape of a drinking vessel, a panda, and two coins. The fruit on the left is peaches.

lumar year. All the women of the family would take turns bowing to the moon. The festival is still held today, but no offerings are made to the moon.

If the weather is good, people sit outside in the evening with their friends and family and enjoy looking at the full moon. They eat mooncakes and drink wine or tea. The children parade through the streets with lanterns.

MOONCAKES

These small cakes in the shape of the moon are the most common feature of the Moon Festival. The cakes are made of pastry filled with bean paste or lotus seeds, and often contain duck egg yolks to represent the moon.

They commemorate an uprising against the Mongols in the 14th century. According to the story a message calling the Chinese to revolt was hidden inside the mooncakes, which were then distributed to the people.

MOONCAKE SONG

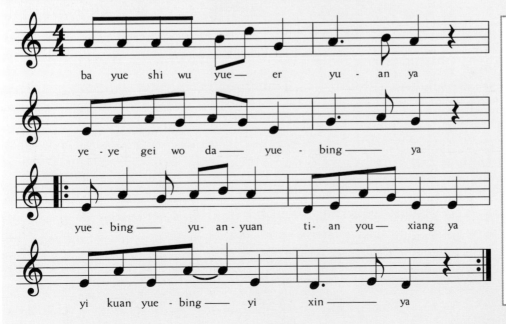

ba yue shi wu yue — er yu - an ya

ye - ye gei wo da —— yue - bing —— ya

yue - bing —— yu- an - yuan ti- an you— xiang ya

yi kuan yue - bing —— yi xin —— ya

It's midautumn and the moon's round, ya. Grandpa is making the mooncakes for me, ya. The mooncake is round, sweet, and delicious, ya. One piece of mooncake, one of heart.

THE MOON LADY
AND THE RABBIT

There are many Chinese legends associated with the moon.

The most popular, and the one that is told and retold at the

Moon Festival, is that of Chang E, the Moon Lady, and how

she came to be condemned to live on the moon forevermore.

CHANG E and her husband Hòu Yi lived in ancient China during the reign of the legendary Emperor Yao. Hou Yi was a member of the Imperial Guard and was also a very skilled archer. He owned a magical bow that shot magic arrows.

One morning, instead of one sun appearing in the sky, there were ten suns. At first the people enjoyed the extra warmth, but it was not long before the heat became too much for them, and the earth began to dry up, and the crops to shrivel. The emperor called Hou Yi before him and ordered him to shoot the extra suns out of the sky. Using the power of his magic bow, Hou Yi shot down the extra suns.

After this great feat Hou Yi's name became famous throughout the land. Even the Queen of the West got to hear of his great skill. She called him to her fairy palace and rewarded him with the pill of immortality. But first she warned him, "You must not eat the pill at once. First prepare yourself through praying and fasting for 12 months."

Since Hou Yi was a careful man, he took her advice. He hid the pill in his house, and began to prepare himself as the Queen had instructed him, with prayers and fasting.

One day while he was away, Hou Yi's wife, Chang E, became curious about a strange smell in the house. She discovered the pill and could not resist swallowing it. As soon as she had taken it, she was able to fly. When her husband returned, she flew out of the window in terror, for she knew she should not have stolen it. Hou Yi raced after her, but she was too fast for him and flew directly to the moon.

When she got to the moon, Chang E found it to be a lonely sort of place. It was empty except for a rabbit under a tree. When she tried to move on, Chang E found that her powers had left her and she was no longer able to fly. Ever since then she has lived on the moon and continued to dodge the magic arrows that Hou Yi shoots at her. Her companion, the rabbit, is always shown pounding the pill of immortality in a large mortar.

CHONG YANG

This festival is based on an old belief that it is unlucky not to climb a mountain on this day.

According to a legend, disaster can be avoided if people leave their house on this day and go to a high place. Chinese people therefore climb hills, towers, and pagodas.

Since the festival takes place in autumn, when the skies are clear but the air is not yet too cold, people often take a trip to the countryside. They may take picnics and drink chrysanthemum wine. Autumn is also considered a good time for flying kites.

This is the season when chrysanthemum shows are held. People take time to admire the beauty of these flowers on this day.

The government has encouraged the association of Chong Yang with the elderly. People make special efforts to pay older relatives respect by visiting and spending time with them.

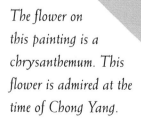

The flower on this painting is a chrysanthemum. This flower is admired at the time of Chong Yang.

26

MAKING A KITE

Kite flying is a very popular sport in China. Kites made from silk, bamboo, and paper are made into all kinds of exotic shapes, including birds, butterflies, dragons, and fish. The decoration of a kite is just as important as its ability to fly. Fighting between kites is also popular. The aim is to cut the string of your opponent's kite. The string is coated with powdered glass to make a sharp cutting edge. When your opponent's kite flies near to yours, you can cut its string and bring it down.

YOU WILL NEED
Flexible cane • Masking tape
Thin paper • Glue
Poster paints
Thin string

1 Take a 40-inch length of cane and bend it into a fish shape. Secure the joint with tape. Then bend two 30-inch lengths and stick them together to form a loop. Tape one on top of other as above.

2 Trace around the outside of the cane shape onto the paper. Paint your design onto the paper. Then, adding 1/2 inch all around the outside to fold over the cane, cut out the paper to the right size.

3 Lay the paper over the frame. Snip into the edges to make them fold over more neatly. Paint glue around the edges, fold over, and stick down. Tie some string onto the frame, and your kite is ready.

MIAO FESTIVALS

The Miao communities of southwest China continue to hold their own traditional festivals quite apart from the festivals held in the rest of the country.

The Miao are the second largest ethnic group in the southwest of China. Altogether there are about seven million Miao. The Miao hold their own festivals, the dates of which are based on the Chinese lunar calendar.

The main feature of Miao festivals is the chance it gives young couples to get to know one another. There is usually a place in every village specially set aside in which boys and girls meet and fall in love by singing to each other.

The Miao are well known for their dancing. The dances are usually performed by the girls to tunes played on bamboo pipes and drums. The pipes are known as *lusheng*. This dance is done in a group and may involve as many as a hundred lusheng. Although the men no longer wear traditional

This beautiful embroidery shows the head of a dragon. The Miao believe the dragon is a kind god who brings blessings to humans.

costume, the women still use it for special occasions. Like all the small ethnic groups in the southwest, they are known for the

28

intricate embroidery on their clothes and the elaborate working on their silver jewelry. Indeed, it is very important for a Miao girl to be

The lusheng *is the traditional* *instrument of the Miao people.* *It is made of bamboo and* *comes in different sizes.*

able to do beautiful embroidery. Everyone believes that a good embroiderer is hard-working and therefore will make a good wife. A girl will start building up a collection of beautifully stitched clothes well before her marriage.

Horse racing and water buffalo fighting are also a usual part of Miao festivals.

As well as elaborate embroidery, *the Miao also wear ornate silver* *jewelry on festive occasions.*

29

OTHER IMPORTANT FESTIVALS

New holidays have been encouraged by the government during the late 20th century. The Chinese have yet to adopt real traditions for these holidays, but many cultural activities take place.

Women's Day (March 8) Working women have the day off. They go on trips or to the movies with their female work colleagues. The men have to go to work as usual. This is an international celebration.

Labor Day (May 1) All working people celebrate Labor Day with a day off.

Children's Day (June 1) Children have a day's vacation from school. They may be taken to films, puppet shows, and other forms of entertainment. This festival is an international one that is celebrated in many countries.

National Day (October 1) The People's Republic of China commemorates its founding in 1949. Everyone has two days' vacation. The day used to be marked by huge parades and performances of dancing. Nowadays the big celebrations are held less often, perhaps only once every ten years.

These masks show how the actors' faces are painted for performances of Peking opera.

WORDS TO KNOW

Altar: A table on which worshipers leave offerings, burn incense, or perform ceremonies.

Ancestor: A relation who lived a long time ago.

Demon: An evil spirit.

Dumpling: A small piece of risen dough cooked by boiling or steaming.

Emperor: A man who rules over an empire. An empire is a country or group of countries ruled by an emperor or an empress.

Ethnic group: A group that is held together by shared customs, language, or nationality.

Immortality: Living forever.

Incense: A mixture of gum and spice, often shaped into thin sticks or small cones, that gives off a pleasing smell when burned.

Lunar calendar: In this calendar a month is the time between two new moons — about 29 days. Chinese festivals are based on the lunar calendar.

Minority: A group of people who are outnumbered by others living in the same region.

Mongols: The people of Mongolia, a country to the north of China.

Pagoda: A tower, usually built as part of a temple, with upward-curving roofs.

Uprising: When people decide not to obey their rulers any more and try to overthrow them.

Yin and yang: The two opposing forces that Taoists believe are found in everything.

Zodiac, signs of: Everyone has their own sign of the Zodiac, based on the position of the stars at the time of their birth. The signs used in China and Japan are different from those used in the West, but they are used for the same purpose — to help people predict the future.

ACKNOWLEDGMENTS

WITH THANKS TO:

China Mainland Store, London, for loan of artefacts p6,16, and 26. Ray Man, Eastern Musical Instuments, London, for loan of *lusheng* p29.

PHOTOGRAPHS BY:

All photographs by Bruce Mackie except: Gina Corrigan/Robert Harding Picture Library p28 and Jane Sweeney/Robert Harding Picture Library p29(right). Cover photograph by Trip/Picturesque.

ILLUSTRATIONS BY:

Fiona Saunders title page, p4-5, Mountain High Maps ® Copyright © 1993 Digital Wisdom, Inc. p4-5. Tracy Rich p7. Debbie Lian Mason p14-15. Susan Moxley (border) p18-19, John Spencer p19. Susan Moxley (border) p24-25, Philip Bannister p25.

SET CONTENTS